UITGAVEN VAN HET
NEDERLANDS HISTORISCH-ARCHAEOLOGISCH INSTITUUT TE İSTANBUL

Publications de l'Institut historique et archéologique néerlandais de Stamboul

sous la direction de

A. A. CENSE et A. A. KAMPMAN

XIII

THE BAR MENASHEH MARRIAGE DEED

THE BAR MENASHEH MARRIAGE DEED

Its Relation with other Jewish Marriage Deeds

BY

SOLOMON A. BIRNBAUM

İSTANBUL
NEDERLAND HISTORISCH-ARCHAEOLOGISCH INSTITUUT
IN HET NABIJE OOSTEN
1962

CONTENTS

THE BAR MENASHEH MARRIAGE DEED

I. INTRODUCTORY

Towards the end of 1952 the first short report on the Murabba'ât discoveries was published [1], together with three very small facsimiles of little fragments. One of these [2] was written in unknown characters. A few pages further on in the same journal there was already a provisional decipherment [3] by the present writer, to whom the editor, Professor S. H. Hooke, had sent a photo with the request for a note about it. The fact that the text was scanty, that it was incomplete on the left and at the bottom and that the investigation had to be carried out without access to the original, made identification of certain letters difficult and was responsible for some errors in the first transliteration (described there as provisional). However, the nature of the fragment as a legal document, and, in particular, a marriage deed, was recognised by him. Further study of the papyrus [4] enabled him to publish a new article with improved readings. [5] Its first part was devoted to a discussion of the letters, in order to establish the text, the second part to dividing this into words [6] and elucidating their meaning.

In Chapter II of the present monograph the text of our document will be subjected to detailed comparison with other Jewish marriage deeds, and the results given in Chapter III. [7]
The 1952 publication [8] had been based on an investigation [9] in which the forms of the letters were compared with those of Hebrew, Nabataean and Palmyrene.

---

[1] G. Lankester Harding, *Khirbet Qumran and Wady Murabba'at*, Pal. Expl. Quart., vol. 84, pp.104-109.

[2] Plate XXVIII, No. 2.

[3] *A Fragment in an Unknown Script*, Ibid., pp. 118-120.

[4] See below footnote 9.

[5] *The Kephar Bebhayu Marriage Deed*, Journ. Am. Or. Soc., vol 78 (1958), pp. 12-18. (Sent to the editor about the end of 1956.)

[6] The division on the papyrus was rarely clear. Almost the only certainty was where a final aleph or final *n* showed a word boundary.

[7] These two chapters were sent to the Editor in November, 1956.

[8] See footnote 3.

[9] Published subsequently: *An Unknown Aramaic Cursive*, by the present writer, Pal. Expl. Quart., vol. 85 (1953), pp. 23-41.

The comparison had revealed a combination of Hebrew and Nabataean elements and yielded an approximate palaeographical date: "round about the second half of the 1st century C.E. or fairly close to it". This date agrees very well with the date, which is given in the text (but not at that time understood by the present writer) and which probably denotes the year 117 of the Christian era. [10], [11]

In 1953, while working on the early centuries of the Square script, he, however, realised that the letter forms on some of the inscribed ossuaries were identical with those of our papyrus. He incorporated this discovery into his work *The Hebrew Scripts* where, of the five facsimiles devoted to this script, the first three are specimens of ossuary graffiti. [12] Until then the palaeographical link between these graffiti had escaped notice, their script had been regarded as simply Hebrew Square like the rest of the ossuary graffiti. This had led, in an extreme case, to the name *'lks'* (Alexa) being read by one scholar as *yw[sp]* (Joseph), and as *yw'mṣ* (Joamaz) by another. [13]

In 1956 a new study of the script was published [14] in which these graffiti were utilised for comparison, as well as two new pen-written finds which had meanwhile been released. [15] The script was — temporarily — designated as the Negeb script because, apart from the graffiti, our material came only from the Dead Sea region, and because the Nabataean element in it points in the same direction. Subsequently two more fragments in that script were found at

---

[10] Cf. Journ. Am. Or. Soc., vol. 78 (1958), p. 15, discussion of Line 1.

[11] In view of the scepticism still persisting in certain quarters as to what palaeography is able to do, this seems to be a striking example of its potentialities: even in such a case as this where the script had first to be deciphered and where there was only a very small quantity of it, the date was correctly established.

[12] When Dr. Milik reviewed the fascicle containing the plate in question he must have overlooked it. Otherwise — when speaking, on another occasion, of the connection between the script of the Murabba'ât papyri and that of the graffiti — he could not have written that it "a été signalé pour la première fois par moi-même en RB LXI (1954) 189; il est repris par BIRNBAUM V.T. l.c., qui cependant omet de citer RB." (Biblica, vol. 38, p. 256, fn. 1, 1957) For that fascicle of *The Hebrew Scripts* was published in **February** 1954, while the issue of the Revue Biblique from which Milik imagined I had appropriated what was his, bears the date **April** 1954 (and, by the way, came out in June or July).

[13] Cf. Vetus Testamentum, vol. 6 (1956), p. 345, fn. 1.

[14] *The Negeb Script*, by the present writer, ibid,, pp. 337-371. Here Milik appears to have overlooked the following passage on p. 338: "By that time I had realised that long before setting eyes on the first Murabba'at document I had actually met with this script elsewhere without being aware of it: among the names scratched on to some of the ossuaries found in the environs of Jerusalem there are a number in this type of writing."

[15] Cf. ibid. p. 342, Nos. 18-22.

Masada [16], *i.e.*, again in those regions. The occurrence of the script on some ossuaries does not suffice to invalidate its ascription to the Negeb because people buried in Jerusalem often hailed from different places. As long as we have no finds indicating the use of this script in a number of regions there does not seem to be sufficient reason to assume that it represents the general cursive parallel of the Square script of the time.

II. COMPARISON

For comparison with our text [17] we have at our disposal three dated papyri from Elephantine [18], a number of short passages from Talmudic literature [19], and, from the middle of the tenth century onwards, many actual deeds as well as specimens in formularies. [20]

Already in Mishnah times the short form of the RK was established. The inclusion of certain clauses was declared unnecessary on the grounds that they were general law. [21] But until late in the Middle Ages one or the other of these clauses was not rarely inserted. Also, special, individual, clauses were sometimes added. Finally such material was put into a separate document. [22] We shall now go through the text, clause by clause.

A. *Good Wishes*

In many RK the text of the deed is preceded by good wishes and/or auspicious quotations from the Bible. This part — short or long — is clearly separated from the text, and is often in a different kind of lettering. Since the upper edge of our papyrus looks as if nothing is missing from it, there seems to have been no such prelude. The EK, too, are without such introductory matter. This does not, however, constitute a link between them and our document, because such a part is by no means of regular occurrence in the RK, either.

---

[16] Bull. Isr. Expl. Soc., vol. 21 (1957), pl. 16, Nos. 3-4.

[17] Designated here by BMK = Bar Menasheh *ktwbh*.

[18] EK = the Elephantine ktwbwt: EK 1 - Brooklyn 2, of 449 B.Ch.E.; EK 2 - Cowley 15, of 441; EK 3 - Brooklyn 7, of 420. Cowley 18, of ca. 425, seems to be a fragment of a marriage deed; Cowley 48, of about 470(?) appears to be a deed of betrothal. (Kraeling, *Brooklyn Museum Papyri*, 1955; Cowley, *Aramaic Papyri*, 1923.)

[19] *Mishnah*: Ket. 4 : 7, 8, 10, 11, 12; Ed. 1 : 12. *Tosephta*: Ket. 4 : 9, 11. *B. Talmud*: Ket. 2 b, 43 b; Qid. 9 a; Naz. 24 a. *P. Talmud*: Yeb. 15 : 2; Ket. 4 : 8, 5 : 8, 9 : 1, 12 : 1; B.B. 8 : 8.

[20] We have designated these documents Rabbinic *ktwbwt* (RK). The list of those assembled and used in the present study is too long to be given here. For the same reason no references to individual deeds can be made or passages quoted.

[21] *tn'y byt dyn*.

[22] Occasionally it is written on the same sheet, side by side with the *ktwbh* proper.

B. *The Date*

As in both the EK and RK, our text starts with the date. As in the EK, it contains no mention of the weekday, which, on the other hand, is regularly included in the date in the RK. It further shares with the EK the direct naming of the month without the addition of the word "month", which, on the other hand, is never omitted in the RK (first *yrḥ* is used, in later times *ḥwdŝ*).

C. *The Era*

After *'srh*, the era was presumably given, as in the EK [23] and RK. If it was the regnal year of the Nabataean king and if the formulae employed in the Nabataean inscriptions were used, it might have been *lrb'l*, *lrb'l mlkh*, *lrb'l mlk nbṭw* or *lrb'l mlkh mlk nbṭw*. If it was the Era of Arabia it might have been *lhprkyh*. From the result arrived at on p. 6 it would follow that only *lrb'l* or *lhrpkyh* are possible here. The latter seems to be the more likely. [24]

D. *Confirmation of the Era*

In the EK the designation of the era is followed by the name of the place, but in the RK this is preceded — especially in later centuries — by a clause expressly stating that the era given is the one employed at the place in question. (This clause is derived from the era clause used for the Seleucid era.) On the basis of our discussion on the length of the line (p. 5 f) we can say that the BMK did not contain this clause; it tallied in this respect with the EK.

E. *The Place*

The name of the place of marriage must have been contained in line 1.

F. *Qualification of the Place Name*

In the EK the place name (Elephantine) is qualified by *byrt'*. Such a short designation is rare in the RK, rarer still is the giving of the name only — as a rule the name of the river (or the sea) where the place is situated is added. In the KBC [25] we have the word *kpr* but it is not a qualification since Bebhayu is a personal name: *kpr* is just part of the name *kpr bbyw*. However, the fact that the word *kpr* is mentioned makes it unnecessary to add it as a qualification even if a qualification was generally in use. There could hardly have been a qualification in BMK, the line not being long enough. (See page 5).

---

[23] E.g., EK 1.
[24] Cf. Journ. Amer. Or. Soc., vol. 78, p. 15.

G. *The Parties*

In this section the EK and RK differ essentially from each other. In the EK the transaction takes place between the bridegroom on the one hand and the bride's father (brother, master) on the other: "Ananiah ... said to Meshullam: I have come to you for you to give me Tamut ... in marriage." [26] But in the RK the bride and the groom are the contracting parties: "X, the bridegroom, said to Y, the bride."

To which of these two types does the BMK conform? From section J, the Marriage Declaration, we shall see that it followed the lines of the RK type. The present section is based on the result we arrived at in that section.

Manasseh is either the name of the bridegroom or that of his father. As it is unlikely that the designation *mn bny 'lysyb* would be appended to his own name and that this would then be followed by his father's personal name, it seems safe to assume that Manasseh was the father's name. [27]

The name of the bride would have followed in the missing part of l. 2. Her father's name might have been qualified by some genealogical designation as in the case of Manasseh (*mn bny 'lysyb*).

The names of bridegroom and bride might have been preceded, as in the RK but in contrast with the EK, by honorifics, and/or followed by the respective designations "bridegroom" and "bride"; the latter might possibly have been preceded by "virgin", "widow" or "divorcee"; the words "bridegroom" and "bride", or their names, might have been accompanied by the demonstrative pronoun; there might have been the verb "he said", possibly preceded by the verb "he came" or by the introductory *'yk* and/or followed by the anticipatory *lh*; or the 1st pers. might have been used, etc.

All these possibilities allow of a great number of combinations. In attempting to reconstruct our text we need first of all to know how long the lines were.

The Length of the Lines

To establish this length we shall start with the first two lines because we know, more or less, what the contents were. We shall first consider the two extreme possibilities — the possible maximum and minimum lengths. If the longest

---

[25] *The Kephar Bebhayu Conveyance* in Palestine Exploration Quarterly, vol 89 (1957), 108-132.

[26] EK 1.

[27] Journ. Am. Or. Soc. 78, p. 17, to Line 16. If that is so then our tentative suggestion that the bridegroom might possibly be the Ḥdr of the KBC, has proved to be untenable. For the name of Ḥdr's father is known to us from that deed — it is Judah and not Manasseh. Nor could Manasseh be the name of the father of Ḥdr's bride, Shalom, because we know he was called Simeon.

possible wording were to result in the roughly equal length of ll. 1 and 2, this could hardly be considered as a coincidence but would give us grounds for thinking that we had arrived at an approximately correct solution. We might further assume that this would be the average length of the other lines, too. If, however, the results for ll. 1 and 2 were to differ greatly, we would have to conclude that one, or both of them, had been incorrectly reconstructed. In that case we would try the same method with the shortest possible wording. If that were to yield a negative result, too, we would have to go on trying intermediate lengths.

The beginnings of the lines are easy to establish. There can be no doubt that l. 1 starts with the date, and that therefore only the two letters $b\dot{s}$ preceded the portion preserved. This right-hand boundary of the writing would be confirmed by l. 13 if — as it seems — there was nothing before the waw.
The longest probable combination would be:

1   $[b\hat{s}]b'h\ l'dr\ \hat{s}nt\ \dot{h}dh\ '[srh\ lrb'l\ mlkh\ mlK\ nb\underaccent{.}{t}w\ lmnyn'\ dy\ rgylynn'\ lmmn'$
    $byh\ b\ldots\ldots\ d'l\ nhr\ \ldots\ldots\ mwtbh\ 'yK\ 't'\ m\ldots\ldots\ \dot{h}tnh]$

2   $[br]\ mn\hat{s}h\ mN\ bny\ 'ly\hat{s}yb\ [w'mr\ lhd'\ \ldots\ldots\ btwlth\ klth\ brt\ m\ \ldots\ldots\ mN$
    $bny\ \ldots\ldots]$

Here l. 1 would have 99 letters while the figure for l. 2 would be 62. In that case either l. 1 would be too long, or l. 2 too short, or our text in both of them wrong.

Now the shortest probable combination:

1   $[b\hat{s}]b'h\ l'dr\ \hat{s}nt\ \dot{h}dh\ '[srh\ lhprkyh\ b\ \ldots\ldots]$

2   $[br]\ mn\hat{s}h\ mN\ bny\ 'ly\hat{s}yb\ 'mr\ l\ \ldots\ldots\ brt\ \ldots\ldots]$

Here lines 1 and 2 are practically of identical length. Hence there seems to be a reasonable likelihood that our reconstruction is approximately correct and that each line had about 32-37 letters. [28]
The shortness of the wording in the initial sections — as demonstrated in this result — links our document with the EK as against the RK. We have already established this connection in section B, and are now able to say that in all probability the same holds good for D, F and G.

H.   *Independence of Will*

In some RK the bridegroom's first sentence consists of a detailed declaration

---

[28] The length of the line would have been roughly 100-110 mm. In the Kephar Bebhayu Conveyance the lines are 145-165 mm long, with an average of 38 letters, the writing being much larger.

that he is acting entirely of his own free will. As l. 3 starts with the next section (J), such a declaration, if there was one, would have to be in the missing part of the previous line. But this has already been otherwise accounted for (see above) so that the BMK would not have contained this section. It is lacking also in the EK and in the majority of the RK. Accordingly its absence here cannot be used for purposes of comparison. [29]

J. *The Marriage Declaration*

The Marriage Declaration of our document is a verbal sentence: *thw' ly l'nth*. This is on the syntactical pattern of the RK: *hw'y/hwy ly l'yntw*. The EK, on the other hand, have a nominal sentence: *hy 'ntty*. Thus the BMK tallies with the RK. The Talmud has both forms. [30]

In the EK the bridegroom not only declares the woman to be his wife but adds *w'nh b'lh*. The absence of this clause in the BMK links it with the RK.

According to these two features the grammatical form of the Declaration corresponds to that of the RK. *Thw'* is therefore in the 2nd pers. — like the *hw'y/hwy* of the RK. This also helps us to read the fragment of a letter at the beginning of l. 3 for which, in our palaeographical examination [31], we had a choice between aleph, zayin, heth or taw: we could now decide in favour of taw, reading *'t* "thou". This would correspond to the use of *'n/l'nh* in some of the RK, and also to the natural stress expressed in the imperative form of the RK. [32]

Hence we are able to say that in BMK the transaction takes place between the bride and the groom.

There is a feature differentiating the BMK from both the EK and RK: Where they have *'ntw* it has *'nth*. That *'ntw* in the EK is, beyond doubt, an abstract noun, follows (a) from the context, e.g., *lmntn ly ltmyt — l'ntw hy 'ntty w'nh b'lh* [33], where the concrete noun (*'ntty*) is clearly differentiated from it, (b) from the term for the marriage contract, *spr 'ntw* [34] where the meaning "wife" is, of course, out of the question. [35]

---

[29] It should be mentioned that we do get this clause in the Kephar Bebhayu Conveyance.

[30] *hry 't ly l'yntw* (Qid. 9a). *lkŝtyknsij lbyty thwyyn ly l'yntw* (J. Ket. 4 : 8). Cf. Tosephta Ket. 4 : 9 (*kŝtykns lbyty th' ly l'ttw*).

[31] JAOS 78 : 12.

[32] EK 1 : 3; parallels: EK 2 : 3-4; EK 3 : 3,37.

[33] Brooklyn 2.

[34] Brooklyn 10 : 7,10; 12 : 18; Cowley 14 : 4; 35 : 4-5.

[35] Accordingly, Lidzbarski's suggestion — for which he adduces no reason — that *'ntw* (in this section) "is an abstract noun but with a concrete meaning — which is a favoured method of designating the female sex" (Ephemeris 3 : 80) is untenable.

Whether the use of *'nth* in the BMK signifies that as this time *'ntw* was felt to be a concrete noun, and that it could therefore be replaced by the normal word for "woman" (*'nth*), it is impossible to say. At first glance it might be thought that the Targumim point towards the concrete meaning, because they sometimes translate *'sh* by *'ntw/'ytw*. However, this is done only where the reference is to marriage, otherwise *'nth/'yth* is used, both words occurring at times in one and the same line. [36] Hence it is clear that the makers of the Targumim simply employed the technical term they were used to from marriage deeds.

K. *kdt*

According to the choice of possible readings suggested in our palaeographical examination for the fourth and third letters from the left-hand edge of l. 3, the last word could be *kdwN, kwwN, KzwN, kywN, krwN, kdyN, kwyN, kzyN, kyyN, kryN*. Most of these sequences make sense by themselves but *kdyN* is certainly the most likely reading, because it corresponds exactly to the *kdt* of the RK. Accordingly, we would expect the next word to be "Moses" — and the traces of the last sign seem to favour this. [37] Thus section *K*, too, links the BMK with the RK.

L. *Invocation*

In the EK the Marriage Declaration is followed by the *mohar* section. In the RK, however, one or more sections intervene.

First we have, in one type of RK, the introductory words *bmymr' dšmy'*, or *bsyy't' dšmy'*, or the combination *bmymr' wbsyy't' dšmy'*. It is impossible to tell whether the BMK might have contained such a section or not.

M. *Promise*

This section is always present in the RK but it is absent from the EK. In it the bridegroom promises to work for his wife, to honour, maintain her etc. If the BMK had such a clause it would have occurred in the second half of l. 3, because l. 4 clearly deals with an entirely different matter. The Promise Formula would have been very short.

N. *Mohar*

Next should follow the *Mohar* clause, as in the EK and many RK: *wyhbt lk(y)*

---

[36] *E.g.,* Gen. 12 : 19 or 20 : 12.

[37] In B. Ket. 72a there is an expression *dt mš wyhwdyt,* and in J. Yeb. 15 : 2, Ket. 4 : 8 we find *lkstyknsy lbyty thwyyn ly l'yntw kdt mšh wyhwd'y.*

mwhr and *wyhbn' lyky mwhr btwlyky,* respectively. But in what we have of line 4, there is no indication of it. However, line 5 seems to speak of money and might thus form the end of the *mohar* clause, the first half of which might have been contained in the missing part of line 4. In many RK the clause ends with the words *dhzw* (*dhzy, dhzn,* etc.) *lyky md'wryt'.* This formula could have been contained in the second half of line 5.

O. *The Bride's Consent*

In the RK the mohar section is preceded or followed by one that records the consent of the bride and the fact that she has now become the man's wife. The EK, naturally, do not have such a section because in them the legal transaction is not between the bride and groom.

It seems there would be no room for it: the end of l. 3 could not have contained more than the words *sby't* and her personal name, so that l. 4 would have to start with the word *brt* and her father's name. But here there is room for only one or two letters. Accordingly, the absence of a Consent Section links the BMK with the EK.

P. *The Bride's Promise*

The same would hold good for the Bride's Promise, which occurs in some of our early RK.

Q. *The Dowry*

This clause should follow on the *mohar* section. If it had been on the lines of the RK the beginning of it could have been contained in the rest of line 5 — something like *wdN ndwny' dy hn'lt ly mN byt 'bwK.* But line 6 would not fit to that.

One might feel tempted to complete the first word of line 4 to read *hn'lt,* on the model of EK and RK. However, the letters after *mN* are not *byt 'bwK.* And then, if the rest of the line were filled by the Dowry clause, where else could we look for space to contain the *mohar* clause?

Qym

The words *lhw' qym* sound like the concluding phrase of a sentence — possibly, here, of a section. They seem to form a sort of final assurance to the mohar and dowry sections. There is nothing of that sort in the EK. In the RK there is an extensive Assurance Clause but it refers to the validity of the deed in general and occurs at its end. [38]

---

[38]   See below, section NN.

R.   *The Bridegroom's Voluntary Addition,*
S.   *His Gift,* T.   *The Total*

These are sections contained in the RK but not in the EK. There is certainly
no room for them in the space of about 21-26 letters available in l. 6. Our Deed
is thus in line with the EK.

U.   *Acceptance as a Loan*

A section of the RK where the bridegroom accepts the previously specified total
as a loan for which he is responsible to his wife, is not represented in the EK.
There is no room for it in the BMK. Its absence cannot be used for purposes of
comparison because such a section is not sufficiently general in the RK.

V.   *The Contingency of the Husband's Death*

The BMK differs from the EK in that it deals first with the contingency of the
wife's — not the husband's — death (see below, section Y). But, like them, it
has a section — beginning in l. 9 — which deals with the contingency of the
husband's death. This is in contrast with the RK. Although in RK the contingency of his death forms the premiss on which the whole deed is based, it is
referred to by implication only: in the words *yrty* or *yrtwhy* or (in a different
type of the RK, where it occurs in another section) by the addition *btr mwty.*
Occasionally the matter forms the subject of an Additional Clause.
Two clauses come under this heading, one concerned with the widow's maintenance, the other with the right of inheritance.

W.   *The Widow's Maintenance*

In the EK there is no clause regarding the maintenance of the widow (apart
from what is implied in her right of inheritance). In the Mishnah we find: *l' ktb
lh 't th' ytbh bbyty wmytznh mn nksyy kl ymy mygd/mygr 'rmlwtk bbyty
ḥyyb ky hw' tn'y byt dyn.* In the RK an Additional Clause is sometimes devoted
to the matter.
Perhaps the *bt* of l. 11 was *bty* "my house", and our passage formed
part of a negatively expressed Maintenance Section: "you cannot be prevented
from living in my house"... The wording *'rmlw* points more in the direction of
the RK than of the EK.

X.   *Inheritance*

In EK 1 and in an Additional Clause of some RK, the wife is declared the husband's heir, without further qualification. In the other EK and in the majority of those RK that refer (in an Additional Clause) explicitly to the contingency of the husband's decease, such reference is restricted to the event of his dying childless.

The final words of l. 11 might perhaps have been completed in this way: *mN bt 'bwk*. A possible inference from the *l'* might then be that this formed part of a provision relating to the disposal of the possessions she had brought from her father's house. However, no such negative clause is known to me from either the EK or RK.

Y. *The Contingency of the Wife's Death*

The section dealing with the contingency of the wife's death must have begun in l. 6, either with the introductory *'m* after *qym* or with another *w'm* at the end of the line. Such a section occurs in EK 1 but not in the RK (clause CC is a special case). Hence the link is with the EK.

In using the idiom "to go to one's eternal home" the BMK differs from the EK, where the plain expression "to die" is employed. But this does not prove greater closeness to the RK because in them this section, when it occurs, is relegated to an Additional Clause, and other verbs (*pṭr, 'dr*) are used: moreover, the Palestinian Talmud, whose form we should expect to tally with the RK, also employs "to die": *'yn mytt bl' bnyn* [39], like the EK.

If *thw'* (l. 3) is the 2nd pers. then it follows that the *h* of *'lmh* (l. 7) does not signify the (fem.) pronoun but indicates the determinate state. That it is not spelt with aleph as in *ṣ̂ṭr'* (l. 14) is not striking: the spelling of these documents is not rigid. [40] The other endings *â* are here spelt with *hê:* [*ŝ*]*b'h, ḥdh* (l. 1), [*y*]*hwd'h* (l. 8), *ŝb'h* (l. 15).

Z. *Burial*

From *thK* (l. 7) onwards until the end of the section the text must have been concerned with the obligations of the husband if his wife should die. The first of these is to bury her. Something to that effect might have been contained in the missing part of l. 7. This duty is mentioned in the Mishnah [41] but there is no reference to it in the EK, nor have we come across it in any RK. Hence such a clause does not seem likely here.

The section ends with [*y*]*hwd'h*. This reminds one of the expression *gwbryN*

---

[39] Ket. 9 : 1, B.B. 8 : 8.
[40] Cf. PEQ, vol. 89 (1957), pp. 131-132.
[41] Ket. 4 : 4.

yhwd'yN in the Promise Section (see M) and *kdt mŝh wyhwd'y* in the Kdt section of J. Yeb. 15 : 2. It suggests a link with the RK as against the EK. This word could have formed part of some such expression as "in accordance with the duty of a Jew", or "as befits a Jew"; it could also have been an adjective qualifying *gbr'* "man" at the end of the preceding line.

AA. *The Inheritance of Sons*

The word *bnN* which, in l. 8 (after the introductory *w'm*) starts a new section, recalls the *bnyN* of the Mishnah passage *bnyN dkryN* [42] (one of the "Unnecessary Clauses"). [43] In view of the text of l. 9, we might think that our passage would tally with the Mishnah. That, however, seems unlikely for these reasons: The wording in the BMK could not have been the same: here the word after *bnN* does not start with *dk;* there is not enough room for a text of that length, the more so as it contains little that could have been cut out.

BB. *Maintenance of Daughters*

The word *bnN* also recalls the Mishnah passage *bnN nwqbN* [44] but various circumstances speak against this identification: the next word starts with *lb* (not *nw* or *nq);* the passage is too long to fit into a line; the text preserved gives no indication at all as to the contents (while in the section AA there was at least the word *[yq]blwN* which made the identification with the passage *bnyN dkryN* feasible); *[yq]blwN* is masc. and cannot, therefore, refer to the word "daughters".

However, even if the clause introduced by *bnN* does not correspond literally to one of the two sections (*dkryN, nwqbN*), it is difficult to overlook the fact that the word occurs in a section relating to the mother's death. This passage may therefore be presumed to speak of her sons' and daughters' rights, the inheritance of her sons and the maintenance of her daughters. The word *bnn* does actually occur in one of the EK [45] but the context is different: the reference there is to children from another wife, while in the KBK we get *bnn*

---

[42] Ket. 4 : 10: *bnyN dykryN dyhww lyky myn'y 'ynwN yrtwN ksP ktwbtyK ytr 'l ḥwlqhwN d'M 'ḥyhwN* (MS Kaufmann has: *dyyhwwN* [correction by another hand], *lyK, dyyrtwN yt*).
[43] Cf. above p. 4.
[44] Ket. 4 : 11: *bnN nwqb(y)N dyhwy(y)N lyky myn'y yhwy(y)N ytbN bbyty wmytznN mnksy 'd dtnsbwN* (Mishnah in Talmud: *dtlqhwN*) *lgwbryN* (MS Kaufmann has: *nqbN, dy yhwwyN lyK, 'ynyN yhwwyN bbyty ytbN;* the P. Talmud has *yhwN ytbN,* omits from *'d* to *lgwbryN* but adds *wmtksyyN bkswty*).
[45] Cowley 15 : 32,33.

in the clause dealing with the wife's death, and the children in question are therefore her own, as in the RK.

If *bnN* means "sons" it would almost certainly be spelt *bnyN*. It may, there-fore, be assumed that this passage deals with the daughters. Hence we might supply the Mishnah text (omitting non-basic words and the doubling of *w* and *y* — in order to keep the line to the required length).

CC. *Childlessness*

If we wanted to connect this *bnN* with a clause about the wife dying childless [46], we would be up against the difficulty that the section in the BMK starts with *bnN*, and no negative is possible before it. Such a clause occurs in EK₂ and EK₃. EK 1 does not have it and it is very rare in the RK (although less rare in the form of an Additional Clause). Hence it is safer to draw no conclusions.

DD. *The Contingency of Divorce*

In Section V we described the contingency of the husband's death — though only referred to by implication — as an unspoken premiss on which the RK are based. There is another unspoken premiss of basic importance: the contingency of divorce. Here, too, the reference is only by implication — in the words *'ly* or *'lwhy*, and *bḥyy*, respectively. In the EK the contingency of divorce is, how-ever, explicitly dealt with.

We would expect the BMK to tally with the EK in this respect as it does in regard to the contingency of death. But there is no evidence in the fragment in support of this. As ll. 9, 11, 13 clearly refer to death it is unlikely that the missing parts of these lines or of ll. 10 and 12 would have dealt with divorce. In this respect it seems that the BMK differs from the EK, and — since there is no room in any other line for such a clause — indirectly from the RK, too.

EE. *Expulsion*

A section about expulsion of the wife occurs in the EK. There is no room for that in the BMK. But since this clause is also absent from one of our three EK, it is safer not to use this feature for comparison.

FF. *Monogamy*

Both in the EK [47] and RK a clause was sometimes inserted in which the

[46] J. Ket. 9 : 1 (*'yN mytt bl' bnyN yh' mdlh ḥzr lbyt 'bwh*).
[47] Brooklyn 7 : 36-37.

bridegroom undertook not to marry a second wife (during the lifetime of his first wife). The size of our deed excludes the possibility of there having been such a section.

GG. *Maid-Servant*

A clause in which the bridegroom undertakes not to force a maid-servant on to his wife if she dislikes her, is occasionally to be met with in the RK. It cannot, for reasons of space, have been contained in the BMK. This clause being very rare in the RK, its absence in the BMK cannot be used for purposes of comparison.

HH. *Captivity*

For reasons of space there is also no likelihood that the BMK contained the RK clause in which the bridegroom promises to ransom his wife if she were to be captured. [48] We do not find it in the EK and only exceptionally in the RK, and it cannot, therefore, be used for purposes of comparison.

JJ. *Religious Reliability of the Bride*

The same reasons of space would apply to a clause in which the bridegroom accepts the complete reliability of the bride in the matter of the $k\hat{s}rwt$ of food, as found — exceptionally — in the RK.

KK. *Undertaking on the Part of the Bride*

Only very rarely was it thought necessary to insert a clause in the RK in which the bride undertook to observe the laws of *ṭbylh*. There would be no room for this in the BMK. Being of only exceptional occurrence in the RK, its absence in both the BMK and EK cannot be regarded as a connecting link between them.

LL. *Divorce on the Part of the Wife*

In the EK we get a clause dealing with the contingency of the divorce of the husband by the wife. This is, of course, impossible in the RK. As our Deed probably contained no divorce clause on behalf of the husband it seems out of the question that there should have been one on behalf of the wife.

MM. *Surety*

The essential clause of the RK is that in which the bridegroom declares that all his present and future possessions will be a surety for the money due to her — the *Mohar*, the Dowry and his Addition. (As mentioned above, no direct

---

[48]   Cf. Mishna Ket. 4 : 8.

reference is made to the contingencies when this would be due, i.e., if he dies
or divorces her.)

The word *'ḥr'yN* which occurs in the RK in this section provides a link with
the BMK (line 12). In the RK this word is the predicate of the sentence. [49]
There is a long form of the clause in the RK where *'ḥr'yN* is followed by *'rb'yN*.
The BMK cannot tally in this respect with the Mishnah text because the
mutilated letters at the end of the line are definitely not *kt*, and there is no
lamedh preceding them. On the other hand, the traces that have been preserved
seem to fit in with the reading *'r*. If correct that would, of course, be the beginning of *'rbyN/'rb'yN* and thus constitute another link with the RK, rendering
the relationship in regard to this clause even closer.

The word before *'ḥr'yN* presumably belongs to the subject of the nominal sentence. *Qn'* would then be the final word of the subject clause. That would not
tally with the Mishnah where the final word is *ly*, the subject clause being *kl
nksyM d'yt ly*. [50] In the corresponding passage of the most common types of
the RK, however, we have a verb from the root *qn'* — obviously the same as at
the beginning of line 12. [51] If we supplied the Mishnah passage we would arrive
at the wording of the RK, but with the omission of all other detail, and that
would just fill line 11: *kl nksyN d'yt ly dy qnyt wdy*. The word *'r[byN]* would
then be followed by *lktbt' d'*. It is, however, unlikely that the words *wlndwny'*,
which usually follow in the RK would have done so in the BMK, because the
beginning of line 13 would then still have contained part of the clause — and
wqwdm cannot belong to it.

The second word of line 13, *yrty*, occurs also in the RK but there it is situated
at the beginning of the Surety section, and it is constructed with *'l*, not *qwdm*.
The contents of this sub-section must, therefore, differ in the BMK and RK.

NN. *Assurance*

The detailed assurance about the validity of the deed which follows in the RK
is not contained in the RK. There could hardly have been room in line 12 for
the Talmudic passage *dl' k'smkt' wdl' ktwpsy dstry* [52], or for even a small pro-
portion of the full wording of the RK (approximately 120 letters — say:
k'ḥrywt kwl ktbt'. For line 13 — which has nothing to do with Assurance —
begins with "and". This shows that the contents of line 13 are a continuation of
what is in line 12 and may still belong to the Surety clause, as suggested by

---

[49] Cf. the Mishnah: *kl nksyM d'yt ly 'ḥr'yN lktwbtyK* (Ket. 4 : 7).

[50] Ket. 4 : 9. MS Kaufmann has *d'ytyN*.

[51] *E.g., mkl špr 'rg nksyN wqnynyN d'yt ly thwt šmy' dqnyty wd'qnh.*

[52] B. Talmud, B.B. 44 b.

yrty. It is not very likely that this passage is a clause of a kind unknown to us from the EK and RK.

Whether the word *ṣtr'* of line 14 could by any chance form part of such an Assurance section it is impossible to say. It would then be separated from the Surety clause. Among the RK such a separation seems to occur only in Hai Gaon's formulary, where the Assurance is incorporated in the next, the Acquisition, clause. That, however, would not be a real parallel as the Acquisition clause is of a general nature while line 13 clearly deals with some specific matter.

OO. *Acquisition*

The next section of the RK records the acquisition by the bride of the rights detailed in the document. The missing part of line 13 could not have accommodated even the minimum essentials of the clause. The preserved part of line 14 does not seem to point to any possible connection with this subject matter, and for the part that is missing the same holds good as for line 13.

PP. *Acquisition from the Bride*

Where the wife undertakes a specific obligation, as in clause KK, there is also an Acquisition section in connection with this. As to the BMK, see under KK.

QQ. *Confirmation Formula*

The text of the RK ends with a confirmation formula: *ṣryr wqyyM,* or (*w*)*hkl ṣryr wqyyM* or *whkl ṣryr wbryr wqyyM*. [53] The EK do not have this. If there was room at the end of line 14, the formula might have been here.

However, there is a confirmation formula in the BMK — the beginning of line 6 — but this can, of course, refer only to the preceding text.

RR. *Scribe's Colophon*

In the EK the text closes with a note by the scribe to the effect that he has written the deed at the order of So-and-So. The RK have nothing similar. [54] In the BMK such a colophon could have formed part of the missing portion of line 14.

SS. *Signatures*

There are no traces of any signatures under line 14. In the Elephantine

---

[53] Cf. in the B. Talmud *ṣryr wqyyM* (B.B. 160 b), in the P. Talmud: *qyyM ṣryr wbrwr* (Git. 9 : 50 c), in both cases referring to a deed other than a *ktwbh*.

[54] The Mishnah passage *ktb swpr w'd kṣr* (Git. IX : 8) seems, according to Gulak, Urkundenwesen, p. 20, to be a vestige of such a colophon.

Papyri [55], the Bar Kosiba Letter [56], the Beth Mashku Document [57] and the Kephar Bebhayu Conveyance [58] the signatures all follow straight under the text on the righthand side (in the Kephar Bebhayu Conveyance, however, the second and further signatures are on the left). The absence of signatures in the BMK is due to the fact that it is not a *gṭ pśwṭ,* a deed in the form of an open sheet (in the Kephar Bebhayu Conveyance we have the actual term *pśyṭ*): see next section.

TT.   *The Double Deed*

That our text is followed, after only a short break, by what is obviously an almost identical text, calls to mind an arrangement to be met with in Greek papyri from Egypt, about the Christian Era. The deed is there written twice on the same sheet, one copy below the other, the top copy signed by the witnesses, rolled, tied up and sealed (*scriptura interior*), the bottom copy remaining open for inspection (*scriptura exterior*).

We cannot tell whether the BMK was rolled or not. However, the photo shows clear evidence of creases. Not all the creases are equally visible but the traces are confirmed by the outline of the fragment: the indentations at the edges are always at both ends of what seem to be the creases, and they are symmetrical on the horizontal axis. The document must have been folded along lines 2, 4, 6, 8, 10, 12, 13, between 14 and 15, above 15, between 15 and 16. (This can be checked by making a tracing of the outline, cutting it out and folding it in accordance with these figures). These creases might have resulted from the rolled deed having been squashed flat — a thing that might easily happen through carelessness or in circumstances when careful treatment was impossible as, for instance, in the course of flight.

The method of closure was different for the *gṭ mqwśr* of the Mishnah. There, a line or two were written, the sheet was then folded at that point and sewn up on the right- and lefthand edges. The BMK cannot have been such a *gṭ mqwśr* otherwise the lines of the text would be separated by blank spaces. Instead, we get each line of the text following the other in uninterrupted succession.

From about the middle of the second century B.C.E. onwards, a new type made its appearance among the Egyptian papyri: the part to be sealed became merely a short summary. It was treated with increasing negligence and badly written, until it was finally altogether omitted.

---

[55]   See above p. 3, note 18.

[56]   Cf. Pal. Explor. Quart., vol. 86 (1954) 23-32.

[57]   *Ibid.,* vol. 87 (1955) 21-33.

[58]   *Ibid.,* vol. 89 (1957) 108-132.

The BMK is not of this type. The top deed seems to be more than a mere summary, and the lettering is as distinct as that of the bottom deed. However, we
do not know to what extent the two texts were identical. Lines 15 and 16 must
either have been shorter than the corresponding lines 1 and 2, or they contained
some additional words, since line 17, *i.e.*, the third line of the bottom deed, starts
with *mN bny 'lyšyb*, while in the top deed these words are near the beginning
of the second line.

III.   RESULTS

a.   *Summary of Comparisons*

Features linking the BMK with the EK:

a.   because they are common to both: — *Y*;

b.   because the BMK and EK differ in the same way from RK: — *B* (weekday), *B* (month), *D, F, G, O, Q, R, S, T, V*.

Features linking the BMK with the RK:

a.   because they tally with the RK: — *J* (transaction), *J* (verbal sentence), *K,
Z, BB, MM*;

b.   because the BMK and RK differ in the same way from the EK: — *J* (*'nh
b'lh*), *W*.

b.   *Conclusion*

This tabulation seems to show that, as far as the contents are concerned, the
Bar Menasheh Marriage Deed stands somewhere between the Elephantine
and Rabbinic Marriage Deeds, just as it stands about half-way between them
in time.

It might be tempting to infer from this that the BMK represents a stage in a
development that leads from the EK to the RK. However, we have no
Palestinian marriage deeds contemporary with those from Elephantine to check
such a theory. But that there is at least an indirect relationship can hardly be
doubted. Perhaps students of law history will be able to throw light on this
matter, as well as on the questions left open in the present study.

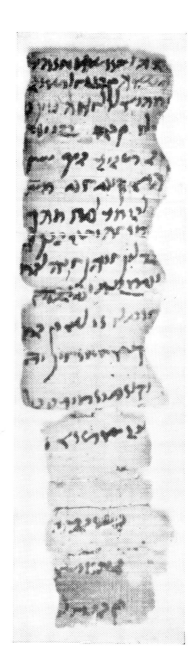

The Bar Menasheh Marriage Document

c. Reconstruction

[בש]בעה לאדר שנת חדה ע[סרה להפרכיה בחד/רד/רו/ינא˙˙˙]	1
[בר] מנשה מן בני אלישיב [אמר ל ˙˙˙˙ ברת ˙˙˙˙ מן ˙˙˙	2
[א]ת תהוי לי לאנתה כדין מֹ[שה וישראל ואנה אזון ואכסה לותכי	3
[ ] עֲלֹת מן נ˙˙ [נ] כֹסֹי ד/רעֹ [ויהבנא לכי מוהר בתוליכי]	4
טֹכ טביע כסף זוזין [מאתן˙˙˙˙˙˙˙˙˙˙˙˙˙˙˙˙˙˙˙˙ [	5
להוי קים אמ תשֹ] הֹ[ן	6
[א]ת לבית עלמה תהדֹ] [	7
[י]הודאה ואמ כנן לה [וין יתכן בביתי־עד די יתנסבן [	8
[ל]בעלין או הן אנה לכת [עלמה אהך את יתבה בביתי [	9
ומתזנה ומכסיא [מן נכסי כוֹל ימין די את יתבה בבית [	10
ארמלו די לא מן בת]˙˙˙˙ כול נכסין די אית לי די קנית ודי]	11
[א]קנא אחראין וער]בין לכתבתיך [	12
וקודם ירתיך מן כול] [	13
לכי שטרא ד]נה [	14
בשבעה [לאדר שנת חדה עסרה להפרכיה [	15
בחד/רד/רו/ינֹא˙˙˙˙ כרמנשה	16
מן בני אלין]שיב אמר ל ˙˙˙˙ ברת ˙˙˙˙˙˙˙˙˙˙˙˙˙˙˙˙˙ [	17

d. Tentative Translation

1. [on the s]eventh of Adhar of the year el[even of the Eparchy, at ......
    ...., ...]

2. [son of] Manasseh of the Sons of Eliashib, [said to ...... daughter of
    ...... of ......:]

3. [Yo]u shall be to me a wife according to the law of M[oses and Israel,
    and I shall provide your food and clothing]

4. .... [and I am giving you the *mohar* of your virginity,]

5. good, coined, to the value of [200] zuz [......................................
..........................]

6. be valid. Furthermore/If [...
.... if]

7. [yo]u go to the house of eternity [...
..........................]

8. [J]ew. And furthermore/if daughters, they shall [dwell in my house until they are taken]

9. [by] husbands. Or if I myself to the h[ouse of eternity go you shall dwell in my house]

10. and will be provided with food and clothing [from my possessions all the time you dwell in the house of]

11. widowhood that [you can?] not [be prevented?] from [living in my?] hou[se. All the possessions I have, those I have acquired and those]

12. [I] shall acquire, are sureties and guar[antees for your *ktwbh* ....
..........................]

13. and before your heirs from all [.....................................
..........................]

14. you th[is] deed [...
..........................]

15. On the seventh [of Adhar of the year eleven of the Eparchy]

16. at .... son of Manasseh

17. of the Sons of Elia[shib said to .... daughter of ....]

Since the preceding paper was written[60], vol. II of *Discoveries in the Judaean Desert* has been published.[61] Here the BMK figures as No. 20. No. 21 is another fragmentary marriage deed, and there are also a number of deeds of sale etc. If photos of all this had been available to the present writer it would have greatly assisted him in deciphering the new script and in elucidating the BMK. In this rich additional material he would have found many specimens of *k* and *z* having the same forms as *b* and *w/y*, respectively. Consequently, his earlier readings in lines 4, 10 and 14 are affected. Moreover, the facsimile of the BMK in the book is clearer than the photo he had at his disposal. On it the *h* at the end of line 8, and the *n*+final aleph at the end of line 16 are illegible. He has accepted the editor's reading of *s* in lines 4 and 5, of ayin in line 9, and of *zwzyN* in line 5. [62] In the light of the new material the present writer has added the following pages. The results arrived at have been incorporated in pages 19-20.

To Chapter I, end (p. 2)

The new material contains four more deeds written in our script and altogether three place names are mentioned in them. The identity of only one of these is certain: Masada, in Mur 19. The fragmentary *'lym* of Mur 29 and 30 is tentatively connected by the editor with the *mdbr yrw'l* north-west of Masada. Mur 28 seems to emanate from *h̄rmnh*, which is identified by him either with *'yr rmwN*, 17 kms north-north-east of Beersheba, of with Rammûn, 18 kms north-north-east of Jerusalem.

The fact that Masada figures in one of these documents supports the original suggestion by the present writer that the new script is connected with the Negeb. *'lym* may point in the same direction, and *hrmnh*, if the identification with *'yr rmwN* is correct, would indicate the same general region.

Among the new material there is one more deed containing our script and bearing a place name. In Mur 24 we have *'yr nḥs*. The editor equates it with the modern *Deir Naḥḥas*, $2\frac{1}{2}$ kms. east-north-east of Eleutheropolis. Although written in the Square script, Mur 24 contains a few letters in the other alphabet. [63] The scribe was obviously a native writer of it. From this it does not

---

[59] of June, 1961.

[60] See above, footnote 7.

[61] Beginning of 1961.

[62] In the footnote on p. 109, the editor refers to the present writer's preliminary articles of 1952 and 1953 but does not mention his further paper in JAOS of Jan.-March, 1958. According to his Introduction (p. 74), he sent in the MS of his book in April, 1958, but worked at it again in the autumn of that year, apart from the bibliography.

[63] The explanation seems to be simple. These letters occur only at the end of a line. The scribe, having arrived near the edge of the column, and wishing to avoid encroaching on the intercolumn more than he had to, changed over to the other script, which is of a narrow type compared with the wide Hebrew Square.

follow that 'yr nḫ̂s was situated in the region where that script was current, but even if it did, the choice of the Square script might be explained by the nature of this particular document: it dealt not with a private but a state trans-action, one party being the Prince of Israel — in such a case the "official" script would be used. For the fact that there is somewhere a regional script in no way rules out the use, on the appropriate occasion, of an "official", or "national", alphabet. This might also explain why the Bar Kosiba Letters [64] and the Beth Mashku Document [65] — possibly, too, Mur 46, of Engedi — are in the Square script.

All this does not provide us with a clear-cut answer to the question as to whether our new script was used in the whole country or was confined to a certain region. But as long as no conclusive material to the contrary comes to light, we may assume that it was the Jewish alphabet of the north-eastern Negeb. It differs from all the later Jewish scripts in that it was not developed from the Square script but was, as it were, a parallel development to it.

To the section: The Length of the Lines (p. 5-6)

The first two lines must include three personal names and one or two place names. The Murabba'ât material now published may give a little additional help towards establishing the length of the lines. It provides us with the average length of personal names during the period in question: three-letter names occur 8 times, four-letter names 42 times, five-letter names 55 times, six-letter names 21 times. From this it follows that we may reckon with an average length of 4.7 letters for personal names of Hebrew origin. Where names are of Greek origin the figure is 6 letters. For place names the result is 5.5 letters. Accordingly we might estimate that the names in lines 1 and 2 occupied about 10-11 and 9-10 letters, respectively.

An examination of the other Murabba'ât deeds [66] in regard to the approximate average number of letters per line yields these figures:

Mur	19	29 letters	(top)	Mur	29	49 letters	
		21	,, (bottom)		30	31	,,
	21	45	,,		32	37	,,
	26	37	,,		KBC	39	,,

---

[64] See footnote 55 and Mur 44.

[65] Cf. Pal. Explor. Quart. vol. 86 (1954) 23-32.

[66] We have left out of account Mur 24 because it is written in Square script which has different measurements and proportions.

The BMK would then belong to a middle group with Mur 26, 32 and KBC, against the smaller Mur 19 and 30, and the bigger Mur 21 and 29.

To section M. *Promise* (p. 8)

Among the many verbs in the Promise sections of the RK, we always find the root *zwN* and often the root *ksh*. They occur elsewhere in the BMK (line 10), and, as they embody two of the three basic duties of the husband, we might expect them to have been used also in the Promise formula (if there was one) of the BMK.

According to most but not all the RK, the formula begins with *w'nh*, a counterpart to the *'t* of the Declaration. Some early RK employ the participial construction *w'hwy z'yyN wmlbŝ* but the general form is *w'yzwN w'ksh* (as also in the formulary of Hai Gaon).

To section W. *The Widow's Maintenance* (p. 10)

The first half of the Mishnah passage would fit in at the end of line 9 and continue at the beginning of line 10 (*wmksy'* being added). The rest of line 10 must have differed somewhat from the second part of the Mishnah, since there is no *bbyty* after the *'rmlw* of line 11. The word *byt* would then have been in line 10 — presumably the last word of it — to form *bbyt 'rmlw*, the possessive pronoun of the Mishnah (*-yK*) being absent. [67] As the texts of Murabba'ât are altogether more simple than the RK, we might think that the BMK did not contain the word *mygd/mygr* and had only *'t ytbh*. In place of *ymy* we would then get *ymyN*, and this form seems to be used in the corresponding passage of Mur 21.

To section Y. *The Contingency of the Wife's Death* (p. 11)

The editor's explanation for his reading of the letter after *m*, in line 7, as an aleph which had begun as a *h* and was transformed half-way through, is unacceptable. An aleph in this position would have to be of the final variety. But what the left part of the letter here resembles is an initial/medial aleph. The whole sign is, however, a *h* — a misshapen one. [68]

---

[67] The editor replaces it by reading *dy lK*. But this does not seem to be a happy suggestion. He calls the letter a kaph "à forme exceptionelle". However, this sign has not the slightest resemblance to a final kaph. It is beyond doubt a final aleph, identical with all the other specimens in this deed.

[68] Cf. JAOS, vol. 78 (1958), 13.

To section AA. The Inheritance of Sons (p. 12)

Mur 21 and 115 both contain this clause [69] so that we might assume its presence also in the BMK. The wording of Mur 21 could be combined with the text of the Mishnah, the missing part of line 7 would then read: *mqdmy bnyK mny yrtwN ksP ktbtyK*. This would fill the line. But there would be no room over for the end of the Mishnah: *ytr 'l ḥwlqhwN d'M 'ḥyhwN*. (The Greek marriage deeds 115 and 116 both contain this part.) Neither would there be any room for such a passage as suggested by us on p. 11 in connection with the reading [*y*]*hwd'h*.

To section BB. Maintenance of Daughters (p. 12)

Instead of the *gwbryN* "men" of the Mishnah we have here *b'lyN* "husbands".

To section MM. Surety (p. 14)

In line 13, the letter after *yrty* is read by the editor as final kaph. Although it differs in form from the specimen in line 8 and from the other specimens in the book, its identification as *K* would enable us to read the next sign as *mN* (as originally done by the present writer, too).[70] But the question as to what this sub-section contained must still be regarded as open.

To section QQ. Confirmation Formula (p. 16)

The other deeds of the volume do not contain such a section, so we may assume that it was absent from the BMK, too, wherein the BMK would tally with the EK.
Instead, the other Murabbaʿât deeds have a closing formula unknown to both the EK and RK: a promise to write a new deed should the other party at any time request it. This would have been included in line 13. The editor restores: *wbzmN dy t'mryN ly 'ḥlP lky ŝṭr'*, on the model of Mur 19.

To section RR. Scribe's Colophon (p. 16)

The other Murabbaʿât deeds do not contain such a clause. It is therefore unlikely that the BMK had one.

To section SS. The Signatures (p. 16)

Both the EK and RK start in the third person: the witnesses report what is

[69] Mur 115, however, tallies with the EK, in that the contingency of the husband's death is dealt with before that of the wife.
[70] Cf. JAOS, vol. 78 (1958), 17 b.

happening. In both there is very soon a switch-over to the second and first persons: the bridegroom's words are reported in direct speech. The EK then revert to the third person and keep to it until the end. The RK add a third change — final reversion to the first person: the witnesses report their participation in the proceedings. The BMK differs from both: here it is only the bridegroom who speaks — except for the first sentence which is probably spoken by the witnesses.

In the EK and RK the document is a report, a declaration by the witnesses, so that it is naturally only they who append their signatures. In Murabba'ât it seems to have been different. To judge by Mur 21, the principals signed before the witnesses. Two of the signatures are followed by the remarks *'l npsh* and *mN npsh,* respectively. We came across the formula *'l npsh* in the Beth Mashku Document and the Kephar Bebhayu Conveyance (and, probably, the Elephantine deed, Cowley 13) after the signatures of the principals in these transactions. We may therefore presume that in Mur 21 these formulae have the same meaning. Accordingly, the missing names which preceded them on the papyrus would have been those of the bridegroom and bride. Mur 19 also points in this direction. It is a bill of divorce where the husband's name is followed by this formula. In addition, there is, we are told, an unpublished Murabba'ât *ktwbh* where *mN npsh s'lh ktb* is appended to the signature of the bride.

On the verso of the BMK there is an incomplete signature. The editor takes it to be that of the bridegroom, no doubt, because it is written at the top edge and must therefore have been the first signature. This would be in line with the unpublished deed just referred to — there the formula after the bride's signature contains the word *ktb.* The same term appears in Mur 21 after a signature (or rather, the hole where the signature had been). We may therefore presume that it was the bride's. From this, in turn, it follows that the *npsh* formula after the first signature (in Mur 21) referred to the bridegroom.

However, if we, accordingly, assume that the first signature of the BMK was that of the bridegroom, then we come up against an insurmountable difficulty. The name of the father here is Jeho[   ] while in the text it is Manasseh. The editor does not mention this problem because he thinks he has solved it by making Manasseh the grandfather of the bridegroom. He states (p. 114) that Mur 18 (not: 14) contains such a double patronymic. But the sign which he reads as *br,* after the father's name, is unlike any of the specimens of *br* in that papyrus (or in any others in the book) and when the man in question appends his signature he gives only his father's name. — The present writer cannot remember any deed giving three generations. We must, accordingly, infer that the bridegroom of the BMK either did not sign — or that if he did, he was not the first to do so. In Mur 21 the scribe signed before the second principal party, the bride, and in the EK before the witnesses. In this connection Mishnah Git.

9 : 8 might be mentioned: *ktb swpr w'd kŝr,* i.e., the scribe of a deed can act as a witness to it. The signature of the BMK, however, is not that of the scribe, the writing being completely different.

To section TT. *The Double Deed* (p. 17)

The evidence of the other deeds confirms that lines 15-17 of the BMK are the beginning of a *scriptura exterior.* In Mur 21 and 28 the top text is shorter than the bottom text; in Mur 19, 22, 25, 29 and 30 the top text is written in smaller writing and the lines are closer together than in the bottom text. This feature corresponds to the later type of the Greek papyri of Egypt (cf. above p. 17). The BMK does not belong to that category.

On p. 17 we have pointed out that the procedure in the BMK must have differed from that followed in the Greek papyri of Egypt, as well as from that in the *gṭ mqwŝr.* The verso of the BMK and the evidence of the other Murabba'ât deeds reveal an additional difference: the signatures are not on the verso of the top text but on that of the bottom text, and they are not written in the same direction as the recto text but at right angles to it. We meet with these features in the Greek deed, Mur 115, too, and generally in the Greek deeds of that period.